WWE

TRIVIA

Fun Facts & Trivia Questions to Find
Out How Much You Know!

By

Steve Pierce

support@bridgepress.org

ISBN: 978-1-955149-90-7

TABLE OF CONTENTS

INTRODUCTION

Professional wrestling is one of the most widely followed sports in the world. Since its inception in the 1800s, fans have been enthralled with the power and strategy of the sport. As with any booming industry, many wrestling companies compete for dominance. One company has not only stood the test of time but continues to stand out from competitors, gaining a cult following worldwide. This behemoth is World Wrestling Entertainment (WWE).

With its history dating as far back as the 1950s, WWE has undergone various name changes before finally arriving at its current trademark. The road to its dominance of the wrestling industry was not a walk in the park. The company faced many challenges, but its legacy has been solidified with consistency, creativity, and hard work.

For decades, the company has produced many household names from its power-packed lineup, created countless memories, and given individuals opportunities to become superstars (as they are popularly called). Some of these superstars even broke into other industries and became global sensations. WWE has also been a platform for other industries' stars to gain further exposure and push them to a higher fandom level.

This trivia book will delve into the rich history of WWE and the present state of the company. This book will help test your knowledge through various sections. These sections include trivia questions in multiple-choice format and true or false. A "did you know" section further enlightens the reader on some interesting facts about the company after each chapter. All of these sections can be found in each chapter of the book.

Whether or not you are a die-hard fan of WWE, this book will undoubtedly provide you with some new knowledge or remind you of some forgotten moments. Either way, you will appreciate remembering or learning.

All information presented below is accurate as of 2021. How well do you know WWE? Let us find out.

CHAPTER 1:

HISTORY AND ORIGINS

TRIVIA TIME

1. In what year did the World Wrestling Federation (WWF) change its name to World Wrestling Entertainment (WWE)?

    a. 2000
    b. 2001
    c. 2002
    d. 2003

2. Which of these was not a former trademark for WWE?

    a. WWF
    b. WWW
    c. CWC
    d. WWWF

3. What family played a significant role in the foundation of WWE?

    a. The McMahon family
    b. The Russo family
    c. The Heyman family
    d. The Wyatt family

4. What era of Professional Wrestling is best known as the "Golden Age"?

   a. The 2000s
   b. The 1970s
   c. The 1990s
   d. The 1980s

5. True or False: The CWC (WWE's earliest trademark) was formerly under the National Wrestling Alliance (NWA) until 1963, when Vincent J. McMahon withdrew the company.

6. Who ended Bruno Sammartino's record-breaking run as champion in 1971?

   a. Dominic DeNucci
   b. Hulk Hogan
   c. Ivan Koloff
   d. André the Giant

7. André the Giant became the top superstar in the whole wrestling industry in the 1970s. In what year did he join WWF?

   a. 1973
   b. 1974
   c. 1972
   d. 1975

8. Hulk Hogan recorded one of the earliest cult followings in WWE history. What name was given to his fan base?

a. Hulkmafia

b. Hulkamania

c. Hulkaship

d. Hulkings

9. Which music star helped the WWF gain widespread attention by joining the company and including superstars in her music videos?

a. Dolly Parton

b. Aretha Franklin

c. Madonna

d. Cyndi Lauper

10. The "Attitude Era" of WWE took place between what years?

a. 1989 – 1992

b. 1991 – 1996

c. 1997 – 2002

d. 2002 – 2007

11. The WWE championship was initially known as the WWWF championship. Who was the first winner?

a. Buddy Rogers

b. André the Giant

c. Antonino Rocca

d. Hulk Hogan

12. Who won the inaugural WWE world heavyweight championship?

a. The Undertaker

b. Triple H

c. Stone Cold Steve Austin

d. Goldberg

13. When did the P.G. Era of WWE begin?

   a. 2008

   b. 2007

   c. 2006

   d. 2005

14. Who won the first-ever WWE championship after WWF became WWE?

   a. The Big Show

   b. The Undertaker

   c. Kane

   d. Triple H

15. In 1963, who became the first-ever president of the then WWF?

   a. Willie Gilzenberg

   b. Roddy Piper

   c. Gorilla Monsoon

   d. Jack Tunney

16. In what year did WWE launch its own 24/7 streaming network?

   a. 2014

   b. 2015

   c. 2016

   d. 2017

17. The "New Generation Era" took place between what years?

    a. 1992 - 1995
    b. 1993 - 1997
    c. 1994 - 1996
    d. 2000 - 2002

18. The "Reality Era" of WWE took place between what years?

    a. 2008 - 2014
    b. 2014 - 2016
    c. 2009 - 2012
    d. 2016 - 2019

19. When did the new era of WWE begin?

    a. 2014
    b. 2015
    c. 2016
    d. 2017

20. Which of these business moguls acquired the rights to one of WWF's biggest rivals, WCW?

    a. Donald Trump
    b. Michael Bloomberg
    c. Ted Turner
    d. Warren Buffett

21. In what country did Buddy Rogers' defeat to Bruno Sammartino take place in 1963?

    a. Argentina
    b. Brazil

    c. Chile

    d. Denmark

22. In what year did WWWF change its name to WWF?

    a. 1979

    b. 1980

    c. 1981

    d. 1982

23. Hulk Hogan was poached from a close rival of the then WWF. What was the name of the company?

    a. Capitol Wrestling Corporation (CWC)

    b. National Wrestling Association (NWA)

    c. American Wrestling Association (AWA)

    d. World Wide Wrestling Federation (WWWF)

24. WrestleMania was created to be a direct rival to which one of these NWA events?

    a. Starrcade

    b. Battle Royale

    c. Monday Night Wars

    d. WrestleFest

25. WWF's collaboration with MTV and other musical acts was known as the?

    a. Rock 'n' Roll Connection

    b. Rock Wrestling Connection

    c. Rock 'n' Wrestling Connection

    d. Music 'n' Wrestling Connection

26. In what year did WWF hit a low point due to

allegations of steroid abuse and sexual harassment?

    a. 1993

    b. 1994

    c. 1995

    d. 1996

27. In 1996, Stone Cold Steve Austin defeated which of these stars to become the king of the ring?

    a. Randy Savage

    b. Jake "The Snake" Roberts

    c. Roddy Piper

    d. Hulk Hogan

28. The incident known as the "Montreal Screwjob" led to which of these superstars leaving WWF?

    a. Vader

    b. Bret "The Hitman" Hart

    c. Randy Savage

    d. Hulk Hogan

29. Following a series of scandals, which of WWF's rivals did stars Hulk Hogan and Bret "The Hitman" Hart defect to?

    a. NWA

    b. WCW

    c. AWA

    d. TNT

30. In what year did WWF entertainment acquire its rival World Championship Wrestling (WCW)?

    a. 2000

b. 2001
c. 2002
d. 2003

ANSWERS

1. C – 2002

2. B – WWW

3. A - The McMahon Family

4. D – The 1980's

5. True

6. C – Ivan Koloff

7. A – 1973

8. B – Hulkamania

9. D – Cyndi Lauper

10. C – 1997 – 2002

11. A – Buddy Rogers

12. B – Triple H

13. A – 2008

14. B – The Undertaker

15. A - Willie Gilzenberg

16. A – 2014

17. B – 1993 - 1997

18. B – 2014 – 2016

19. C – 2016

20. C – Ted Turner

21. B - Brazil

22. A – 1979

23. C - American Wrestling Association (AWA)

24. A – Starrcade

25. C - Rock 'n' Wrestling Connection

26. A – 1993

27. B - Jake "The Snake" Roberts

28. B - Bret "The Hitman" Hart

29. B - WCW

30. B - 2001

DID YOU KNOW?

- The World Wrestling Federation (WWF) had to change its name to World Wrestling Entertainment after losing a lawsuit to the World Wildlife Fund. Because of this, they could no longer use the "WWF" trademark.

- On May 4th, 2002, Insurrextion became the last WWF branded pay-per-view event.

- Capitol Wrestling Corporation (CWC) was the earliest name used by the wrestling body. Its use went as far back as 1953.

- Jess and Vince J. McMahon are both credited as the founding fathers of the wrestling federation.

- Vincent J McMahon renamed Capitol Wrestling Corporation (CWC) as World Wide Wrestling Federation (WWWF) in 1963.

- WWE superstars are no longer allowed to bleed in the ring. The ban was put in place in 2008 to make WWE suitable for more audiences.

CHAPTER 2:

WWE RECORDS

TRIVIA TIME

1. Which superstar has won the most WWE championships?
    a. The Undertaker
    b. Brock Lesnar
    c. Triple H
    d. John Cena

2. How long did the fastest match in WWE history last?
    a. Three seconds
    b. Four seconds
    c. Five seconds
    d. Six seconds

3. What are the longest singles match in WWE history?
    a. Hulk Hogan vs. André the Giant
    b. Bruno Sammartino vs. Waldo Von Erich
    c. The Rock vs. Goldberg
    d. Shawn Michaels vs. The Undertaker

4. What superstar has fought in the most matches?
    a. Randy Orton

b. Dolph Ziggler

c. The Big Show

d. Kane

5. Who is the youngest wrestler to become a WWE champion?

   a. Shawn Michaels

   b. Daniel Bryan

   c. Brock Lesnar

   d. The Rock

6. True or False: Koffi Kingston is the first superstar born in the continent of Africa to win the WWE title.

7. Who is the oldest wrestler to become a WWE champion?

   a. Goldberg

   b. Sting

   c. Vince McMahon

   d. Kane

8. Which superstar was the youngest to become the World Heavyweight Champion?

   a. Randy Orton

   b. Brock Lesnar

   c. John Cena

   d. Rey Mysterio

9. What superstar had the shortest reign as World Champion?

   a. André the Giant

   b. The Rock

   c. Ric Flair

d. Stone Cold Steve Austin

10. True or False: John Cena has the most WWE championship reigns with thirteen.

11. Who is the longest-reigning World Heavyweight Champion?

    a. Triple H
    b. Brock Lesnar
    c. The Undertaker
    d. Batista

12. Bruno Sammartino holds the record for the longest WWE Championship reign. How long did it last?

    a. Six years, ten months
    b. Eight years, six months
    c. Seven years, eight months
    d. Nine years, eight months

13. Who is the oldest World Heavyweight Champion?

    a. The Undertaker
    b. Vince McMahon
    c. Triple H
    d. Ric Flair

14. What team has the most WWE Tag Team Championship reigns?

    a. Edge and Christian
    b. Hardy Boyz
    c. The Dudley Boyz
    d. Harlem Heat

15. Which superstar has won the most Tag Team Championships with twelve?

    a. Christian
    b. Chris Jericho
    c. Edge
    d. Shawn Michaels

16. Which superstar has the most Royal Rumble wins?

    a. Batista
    b. Randy Orton
    c. John Cena
    d. Stone Cold Steve Austin

17. Which superstar has the most combined eliminations in Royal Rumble matches?

    a. Braun Strowman
    b. Kane
    c. Randy Orton
    d. Stone Cold Steve Austin

18. Which superstar has the longest reign as the WWE United States Champion?

    a. Bobby Lashley
    b. M.V.P.
    c. Dean Ambrose
    d. AJ Styles

19. Which superstar has won the most WWE Intercontinental Championship titles?

    a. Chris Jericho
    b. Big E Langston

c. Randy Savage
d. Pedro Morales

20. Which superstar holds the longest reign as Intercontinental Champion?

    a. Big E Langston
    b. Chris Jericho
    c. The Honky Tonk Man
    d. Don Muraco

21. What is the longest ever WWE PPV event?

    a. Royal Rumble 2011
    b. Hell in a Cell 2006
    c. T.L.C. 2015
    d. Money in the Bank 2010

22. What is the longest ever Tag Team match in Federation history?

    a. Shawn Michaels and Triple H vs. Kane and The Undertaker
    b. Mr. Fuji & Professor Toru Tanaka vs. Chief Jay Strongbow and Sonny King
    c. Chris Jericho and Edge vs. Randy Orton and Batista
    d. The Dudley Boyz vs. The Hardy Boys

23. Which superstar has the most WWE World Heavyweight Championship reigns?

    a. The Undertaker
    b. Brock Lesnar

c. Edge

d. Randy Orton

24. Which superstar has the highest PPV matches in WWE history?

    a. Kane

    b. The Big Show

    c. John Cena

    d. The Undertaker

25. Which superstar has the most WWE Championship reigns?

    a. Ric Flair

    b. John Cena

    c. Brock Lesnar

    d. Shawn Michaels

26. Which superstar has the shortest WWE World Heavyweight Championship reign?

    a. Kane

    b. The Big Show

    c. The Undertaker

    d. Triple H

27. Which WWE Diva has the most reigns as WWE Women's Champion?

    a. Trish Stratus

    b. The Fabolous Moolah

    c. Mickie James

    d. Layla

28. True or False: The Fabolous Moolah is the oldest

woman in the history of the company to win a title at 76 years and 7 days.

29. Which WWE Diva has the record of the shortest reign as WWE Women's Champion?

    a. Wendi Richter
    b. Mickie James
    c. AJ Lee
    d. Nikki Bella

ANSWERS

1. A – John Cena

2. A – Three seconds, Chris Jericho and Jerry Lawler defeated Tazz and Naked Mideon

3. B - Bruno Sammartino vs. Waldo Von Erich (81 minutes)

4. D - Kane

5. C – Brock Lesnar

6. True

7. C – Vince McMahon

8. A – Randy Orton

9. A – André the Giant

10. True

11. D – Batista

12. C – Seven years, eight months

13. A- The Undertaker

14. C – The Dudley Boyz

15. C – Edge

16. D - Stone Cold Steve Austin

17. B – Kane

18. C – Dean Ambrose

19. A – Chris Jericho

20. C – The Honky Tonk Man

21. A - Royal Rumble 2011

22. B – Mr. Fuji & Professor Toru Tanaka vs. Chief Jay Strongbow and Sonny King

23. C – Edge

24. D – The Undertaker

25. B – John Cena (10)

26. B - The Big Show (one minute, fifty-two seconds)

27. A – Trish Stratus

28. True

29. B – Mickie James

DID YOU KNOW?

- The Undertaker is the longest-serving member of WWE in history, having worked with the company for thirty years, not so closely followed by The Big Show, who has served for twenty-one years.

- Some of the other long-serving members include John Cena, Randy Orton, and R-Truth.

- John Cena holds the record for most WWE matches won with well over a thousand wins since his 2002 debut. He also has the highest win percentage in pay-per-view matches with a percentage of around 66%.

- Koffi Kingston, Randy Orton, and Kane are also part of the superstars with the highest WWE history wins.

- There are twenty-nine superstars with over 400 wins in WWE.

CHAPTER 3:

SIGNATURE MOVES AND FINISHERS

TRIVIA TIME

1. "Spear" is a move best known for its use by which of these superstars?

    a. CM Punk
    b. Edge
    c. Christian
    d. Chris Jericho

2. Which of these moves was popularized by The Undertaker?

    a. Brogue Kick
    b. Tombstone Piledriver
    c. Body Drop
    d. Sledgehammer

3. The move "Attitude Adjustment" belongs to what superstar?

    a. Shane McMahon
    b. Chavo

c. Rey Mysterio

d. John Cena

4. The "Choke Slam" is a move frequently used by all but one of these superstars.

   a. Kane

   b. The Undertaker

   c. Sheamus

   d. Big Show

5. Which of these two moves was used by Hulk Hogan as his signature?

   a. Leg Drop and Axe Bomber

   b. Choke Slam and Tombstone Piledriver

   c. Attitude Adjustment and Ankle Lock

   d. Frog Splash and R.K.O

6. The "F5" is currently one of the most potent finishers in WWE. What superstar uses the move?

   a. Roman Reigns

   b. Brock Lesnar

   c. Seth Rollins

   d. Dean Ambrose

7. The "People's Elbow" is a move used by which wrestler?

   a. The Rock

   b. Hulk Hogan

   c. Shawn Michaels

   d. Steve Austin

8. Which of these superstars popularized the move "Ankle Lock"?

    a. Ric Flair
    b. Kurt Angle
    c. Batista
    d. Mark Henry

9. True or False: The "Five-Star Frog Splash" was a modification to "The Frog Splash" by Rob van Dam.

10. True or False: "Stone Cold Stunner" is a move accredited to Goldberg.

11. "Jackhammer" is a move that was used by which of these retired superstars?

    a. Goldberg
    b. Steve Austin
    c. The Rock
    d. The Undertaker

12. "Sister Abigail" is a move used by which of these superstars?

    a. Eric Rowen
    b. Luke Harper
    c. Seth Rollins
    d. Bray Wyatt

13. The "Sweet Chin Music" was a move used by which of these stars?

    a. Triple H
    b. Shawn Michaels

c. Kane

d. Booker T

14. The move "R.K.O." is a finisher by Randy Orton and also the initials of his name. What does the "K" stand for?

a. Kyle

b. Kevin

c. Keith

d. Kyrie

15. "619" is a finisher popularly used by which of these superstars?

a. Chavo Guerrero

b. Rey Mysterio

c. John Cena

d. Shane McMahon

16. Which of these superstars makes use of the finisher "Brogue Kick"?

a. Sheamus

b. Antonio Cesaro

c. Drew McIntyre

d. Titus O'Neil

17. True or False: Roman Reigns invented "Suplex City."

18. Which superstar popularized the "Twist of Fate"?

a. Matt Hardy

b. Sting

c. Randy Orton

d. Jeff Hardy

19. The "Mandible Claw" is a move used by which of these superstars?

    a. Abyss
    b. Mick Foley
    c. Kane
    d. Ultimate Warrior

20. Which of these superstars use the "Scissors Kick" as their signature move?

    a. Booker T
    b. R-Truth
    c. Koffi Kingston
    d. Big E Langston

21. The "Samoan Spike" is a finisher credited to whom?

    a. Roman Reigns
    b. Jimmy Uso
    c. Samoa Joe
    d. Umaga

22. Which of these superstars uses "Wasteland" as their finishing move?

    a. Wade Barett
    b. Jeff Jarett
    c. CM Punk
    d. Daniel Bryan

23. True or False: "The Power of the Punch" is a finishing move used by William Regal.

24. The "G.T.S." is a move notable for its use by which of these superstars?

    a. Dolph Ziggler
    b. CM Punk
    c. John Cena
    d. Randy Orton

25. Which of these superstars uses the move "Pedigree" as his finisher?

    a. Shawn Michaels
    b. Ric Flair
    c. Batista Bomb
    d. Triple H

26. Which WWE group made use of the "Triple Powerbomb" as their finisher?

    a. S.H.I.E.L.D
    b. Nexus
    c. New Day
    d. D Generation X

27. "Shell Shocked" is a move used by which of these superstars?

    a. Ryback
    b. Antonio Cesaro
    c. Big E Langston
    d. Kevin Owen

28. Which of these superstars made use of "The Neutralizer" as his finishing move?

a. The Miz

b. Fandango

c. Antonio Cesaro

d. Alberto Del Rio

29. The world's strongest slam is a move used by which of these superstars?

    a. Big Show

    b. André the Giant

    c. Great Khali

    d. Mark Henry

30. Which WWE diva uses "The Figure-eight" as her finisher?

    a. Becky Lynch

    b. Charlotte Flair

    c. Ronda Rousey

    d. Brie Bella

ANSWERS

1. B - Edge

2. B - Tombstone Piledriver

3. D - John Cena

4. C - Sheamus

5. A - Leg drop and Axe Bomber

6. B - Brock Lesnar

7. A - The Rock

8. B - Kurt Angle

9. True

10. False

11. A - Goldberg

12. D - Bray Wyatt

13. B - Shawn Michaels

14. C – Keith

15. B – Rey Mysterio

16. A – Sheamus

17. False - Brock Lesnar originated Suplex City

18. D – Jeff Hardy

19. B – Mick Foley

20. A – Booker T

21. D – Umaga

22. – Wade Barett

23. True

24. B – CM Punk

25. D – Triple H

26. A - S.H.I.E.L.D

27. A – Ryback

28. C – Antonio Cesaro

29. D – Mark Henry

30. B – Charlotte Flair

DID YOU KNOW?

- In 1997 the "Piledriver" was banned as a move after Owen Hart accidentally used it to cause an injury to rising star Stone Cold Steve Austin. Since then, the move has been used by The Undertaker and Kane, who were given special permission by the WWE to use slightly safer versions.

- Randy Orton no longer uses the "Punt Kick" as his finishing move. The company considered this move to be too dangerous for his opponents.

CHAPTER 4:

NICKNAMES/RINGNAMES

TRIVIA TIME

1. "Heartbreak Kid" (H.B.K.) is a name associated with which WWE legend?

    a. Bret Hart
    b. Shawn Michaels
    c. Chris Jericho
    d. John Morrison

2. What superstar is also known as "The Nature Boy"?

    a. Booker T
    b. Finlay
    c. Ric Flair
    d. Rey Mysterio

3. True or False: Triple H is also known as "The King of Kings."

4. Which WWE Diva is known as "The Man"?

    a. Becky Lynch
    b. Rhonda Rousey
    c. Charlotte Flair
    d. Stephanie McMahon

5. Dave Bautista is also known as?

    a. The Animal

    b. The Monster

    c. The Dog

    d. The King

6. Which superstar is also known as The Viper?

    a. Edge

    b. Christian

    c. Sting

    d. Randy Orton

7. Which WWE legend is popularly known as "The Hit Man"?

    a. The Rock

    b. Steve Austin

    c. Ultimate Warrior

    d. Bret Hart

8. What superstar was popularly referred to as "The Best in the World" by himself and fans?

    a. CM Punk

    b. John Cena

    c. The Miz

    d. Mr. Kennedy

9. The "Big Red Monster" is another name for which superstar?

    a. The Undertaker

    b. The Big Show

    c. Mankind

    d. Kane

10. Which WWE Diva is popularly known as "The Queen"?

    a. AJ Lee
    b. Charlotte Flair
    c. Becky Lynch
    d. Brie Bella

11. "The American Dragon" is a nickname for which of these superstars?

    a. Daniel Bryan
    b. Luke Harper
    c. Finn Balor
    d. Roman Reigns

12. Which superstar is popularly known as the "Rated R Superstar"?

    a. Chris Jericho
    b. Christian
    c. Edge
    d. Randy Orton

13. "The Architect" is a nickname for which of these superstars?

    a. Triple H
    b. Dean Ambrose
    c. Bray Wyatt
    d. Seth Rollins

14. True or False: Dolph Ziggler is the wrestler popularly

known as "The Showoff."

15. Which superstar is famously known as "The Lunatic Fringe"?

    a. Dean Ambrose
    b. Seth Rollins
    c. Roman Reigns
    d. Bray Wyatt

16. Which superstar did the late Eddie Guerrero feud with for the name "The Lord of the Ring"?

    a. Chris Benoit
    b. Chavo Guerrero
    c. Rey Mysterio
    d. Diamond Dallas Page

17. Which superstar is popularly known as "The Fiend"?

    a. Bray Wyatt
    b. Eric Rowen
    c. Luke Harper
    d. Goldust

18. Which superstar is known as "The All-American American"?

    a. Jim Morrison
    b. Kurt Angle
    c. Jack Swagger
    d. Hulk Hogan

19. Which superstar is known as "The Ayatollah of Rock and Rolla"?

a. Chris Jericho
b. Christian
c. Edge
d. The Rock

20. Which WWE legend is known as "The Blade Runner Flash"?

    a. Ultimate warrior
    b. Sting
    c. Edge
    d. Randy Savage

21. Which superstar is known as the "Bionic Redneck"?

    a. Goldberg
    b. Stone Cold Steve Austin
    c. Kurt Angle
    d. Kane

22. Which WWE Legend is also called "The 8th Wonder of the World"?

    a. Great Khali
    b. Mark Henry
    c. André the Giant
    d. The Big Show

23. Which WWE Legend is popularly known as "The Deadman"?

    a. Mankind
    b. Kane
    c. The Fiend

d. The Undertaker

24. Which WWE Diva is popularly called "Glamazon"?

    a. Beth Phoenix
    b. Vicky Guerrero
    c. Stephanie McMahon
    d. AJ Lee

25. Which WWE superstar is popularly known as "The Champ"?

    a. Randy Orton
    b. John Cena
    c. CM Punk
    d. Triple H

26. Which WWE Legend is known as "The Excellence of Execution"?

    a. Ultimate Warrior
    b. Bret "The Hitman" Hart
    c. Jimmy Hart
    d. Hulk Hogan

27. Which WWE Legend was popularly known as "The Living Legend" during his time with the federation?

    a. André the Giant
    b. Hulk Hogan
    c. Bruno Sammartino
    d. The Undertaker

28. Who is known as "The Mouth from the South"?

    a. Kevin Owens

b. The Rock

c. Mr. Anderson

d. Jimmy Hart

29. Which superstar is known as "The Funkasarus"?

    a. Tyler Sweet

    b. Aron Stevens

    c. Brodus Clay

    d. Bobby Lashley

30. Who is the "Samoan Bulldozer"?

    a. Umaga

    b. Jimmy Uso

    c. Jay Uso

    d. Samoa Joe

ANSWERS

1. B - Shawn Michaels

2. C - Ric Flair

3. True

4. A - Becky Lynch

5. A - The Animal

6. D - Randy Orton

7. D - Bret Hart

8. A - CM Punk

9. D - Kane

10. B - Charlotte Flair

11. A - Daniel Bryan

12. C - Edge

13. D - Seth Rollins

14. True

15. A - Dean Ambrose

16. D - Diamond Dallas Page

17. A - Bray Wyatt

18. C – Jack Swagger

19. A – Chris Jericho

20. B - Sting

21. B – Stone Cold Steve Austin

22. C – André the Giant

23. D – The Undertaker

24. A – Beth Phoenix

25. B – John Cena

26. B - Bret "The Hitman" Hart

27. C - Bruno Sammartino

28. D - Jimmy Hart

29. C – Brodus Clay

30. A – Umaga

DID YOU KNOW?

- WWE ring names vary. While some superstars go by made-up names, a few others go by their biological names.

CHAPTER 5:

POPULAR CATCHPHRASES

TRIVIA TIME

1. Complete the following sentence: "If ya smell what the rock is _____."

   a. Baking
   b. Eating
   c. Cooking
   d. Roasting

2. "You can't see me" is a catchphrase popularized by which of these superstars?

   a. Randy Orton
   b. Ric Flair
   c. John Cena
   d. Rey Mysterio

3. Complete the following, "Woo, woo, woo, _____."

   a. You know it
   b. You got it
   c. You own it
   d. You show it

4. Complete the following, "I'm the Miz, and I'm ___."

a. Perfect

b. Awesome

c. Superb

d. Fantastic

5. Saying "Yes! Yes! Yes!" repeatedly was popularized by which of these superstars?

   a. Ted Dibiase

   b. Daniel Bryan

   c. The Miz

   d. Jack Swagger

6. Which WWE superstar is known for saying, "Can you dig that, sucka"?

   a. Booker T

   b. R-Truth

   c. Big E Langston

   d. Koffi Kingston

7. Which WWE Diva made frequent use of the phrase "Excuse Me!" She also served as an executive.

   a. Stephanie McMahon

   b. Vicky Guerrero

   c. Charlotte Flair

   d. AJ Lee

8. Which WWE Superstar used the catchphrase "I spit on the face of people who don't want to be cool"?

   a. Chavo Guerrero

   b. Alberto Del Rio

    c. Carlito

    d. Chris Benoit

9. Which superstar popularized the catchphrase "What's up"?

    a. R-Truth

    b. Booker T

    c. Seth Rollins

    d. Goldberg

10. Which WWE Legend is known to say, "Give me a hell, yeah"?

    a. Goldberg

    b. Hulk Hogan

    c. Ric Flair

    d. Stone Cold Steve Austin

11. Which superstar popularized the phrase "Rest in Peace"?

    a. Kane

    b. The Big Show

    c. Mankind

    d. The Undertaker

12. Complete the following catchphrase: "And that's the bottom line 'cause _____ said so."

    a. Goldberg

    b. Stone Cold Steve Austin

    c. The Rock

    d. Vince McMahon

13. Which Legendary WWE tag team popularized the two words "suck it"?

    a. D Generation X
    b. Dudley boys
    c. Hardy Boys
    d. The New Day

14. Complete the following: "What you gonna do when the _____ runs wild on you"?

    a. Animal
    b. Game
    c. H.B.K.
    d. Hulkamania

15. Which superstar popularized the catchphrase "Woo"?

    a. Dolph Ziggler
    b. Ric Flair
    c. Stone Cold Steve Austin
    d. J.B.L.

16. Which WWE announcer/ringside commentator popularized the catchphrase "And, I quote"?

    a. Jerry Lawler
    b. King Booker
    c. Michael Cole
    d. M.V.P.

17. Which WWE Legend popularized the catchphrase "I'm the Best There Is, the Best There Was and the Best There Ever Will Be"?

a. Bret "The Hitman" Hart
b. Jimmy Hart
c. Hulk Hogan
d. Stone Cold Steve Austin

18. Which WWE executive is known for frequently saying "You're fired"?

a. Triple H
b. Vince McMahon
c. Shane McMahon
d. Stephanie McMahon

19. Which WWE superstar popularized the catchphrase "Testify"?

a. Bubba Ray Dudley
b. D-Von Dudley
c. Big E Langston
d. Bray Wyatt

20. Which superstar popularized the catchphrase "boom boom boom"?

a. Koffi Kingston
b. R-Truth
c. Ryback
d. Sheamus

21. Which superstar made use of the phrase "I am a wrestling god"?

a. Shawn Michaels

b. Triple H

c. The Undertaker

d. J.B.L.

22. Which superstar makes use of the catchphrase "Ain't I great"?

a. Jeff Jarrett

b. Bad news Barrett

c. The Miz

d. R-Truth

23. Complete this catchphrase: "And you will know that Austin 3:16 means I just whooped your_____."

a. Face

b. Body

c. Backside

d. Ass

24. Which WWE superstar uses the catchphrase "To be the man you gotta beat the man"?

a. The Rock

b. Stone Cold Steve Austin

c. Ric Flair

d. Triple H

25. Which famous tag team uses the catchphrase "For the benefit of those with flash photography"?

a. D Generation X

b. Edge and Christian

c. The Miz and John Morison

d. The Hardy Boys

26. Which WWE superstar uses the catchphrase "It's true"?

    a. R-Truth
    b. Kurt Angle
    c. Mr. Anderson
    d. Daniel Bryan

27. Which WWE superstar popularized the catchphrase "Hello ladies"?

    a. Val Venis
    b. Ric Flair
    c. Dusty Rhodes
    d. Shawn Michaels

28. Which WWE superstar uses the catchphrase "The champ is here" to announce his presence?

    a. Randy Orton
    b. The Rock
    c. John Cena
    d. CM Punk

29. Which WWE superstar says, "I am the best in the world"?

    a. CM Punk
    b. John Cena
    c. JBL
    d. The Rock

30. Which WWE group leader popularized the catchphrase "Follow the buzzer"?

    a. Roman Reigns
    b. Bray Wyatt

c. Triple H
d. The Undertaker

ANSWERS

1. C – Cooking

2. C – John Cena

3. A – You know it

4. B – Awesome

5. B – Daniel Bryan

6. A – Booker T

7. B – Vicky Guerrero

8. C – Carlito

9. A – R-Truth

10. D – Stone Cold Steve Austin

11. D – The Undertaker

12. B – Stone Cold Steve Austin

13. A – D Generation X

14. D – Hulkamania

15. B – Ric Flair

16. C – Michael Cole

17. A - Bret "The Hitman" Hart

18. B - Vince McMahon

19. B - D-Von Dudley

20. A - Koffi Kingston

21. D – JBL

22. A – Jeff Jarett

23. D – Ass

24. C – Ric Flair

25. B – Edge and Christian

26. B – Kurt Angle

27. A – Val Venis

28. C – John Cena

29. A – CM Punk

30. B – Bray Wyatt

DID YOU KNOW?

- WWE Fans created and popularized the catchphrases "this is awesome" and "you suck." The former is used to show pleasure about something they have just witnessed, while the latter is used to show discontent with something.

- Unique catchphrases are an essential part of WWE, and each superstar has at least one catchphrase. Stone Cold Steve Austin, The Rock, and John Cena have multiple famous slogans due to their eccentricity on the microphone.

CHAPTER 6:

WRESTLEMANIA

TRIVIA TIME

1. The first WrestleMania took place in what year?
    a. 1982
    b. 1983
    c. 1984
    d. 1985

2. True or False: There has only ever been one steel cage main event held at WrestleMania.

3. What superstar has the most wins at WrestleMania?
    a. Triple H
    b. Hulk Hogan
    c. Undertaker
    d. Kane

4. Which of these famous boxers served as a guest referee at WrestleMania?
    a. Mike Tyson
    b. Muhammad Ali
    c. George Foreman
    d. Vladimir Klitschko

5. What superstar has the most losses at WrestleMania?

    a. Triple H
    b. Kane
    c. John Cena
    d. The Big Show

6. Which superstar has the longest unbeaten streak at WrestleMania?

    a. Hulk Hogan
    b. The Undertaker
    c. Triple H
    d. Ric Flair

7. How many editions of WrestleMania have taken place?

    a. 33
    b. 34
    c. 35
    d. 36

8. Which superstar worked the most matches on a single WrestleMania match night?

    a. Randy Savage
    b. The Undertaker
    c. Shawn Michaels
    d. Bret "The Hitman" Hart

9. Which WWE Legend has featured in the most WrestleMania main event matches?

    a. Hulk Hogan
    b. The Undertaker

    c. Randy Orton

    d. Brock Lesnar

10. The longest ever WrestleMania match took place between what wrestlers?

    a. Triple H vs. The Undertaker

    b. Bret "The Hitman" Hart vs. Shawn Michaels

    c. Brock Lesnar vs. Roman Reigns

    d. Triple H vs. Shawn Michaels

11. How long did the longest ever WrestleMania match last?

    a. Thirty Minutes

    b. One Hour

    c. Two Hours

    d. Three Hours

12. Which WWE Legend has worked the most WrestleMania matches?

    a. Kane

    b. The Undertaker

    c. André the Giant

    d. Hulk Hogan

13. This boxer served as an enforcer at WrestleMania.

    a. Anthony Joshua

    b. Tyson Fury

    c. Mike Tyson

    d. Muhammad Ali

14. In what month of the year does WrestleMania currently take place?

    a. December
    b. August
    c. April
    d. October

15. True or False: WrestleMania 2 is the only WrestleMania event that took place on a Monday.

16. Where was the first-ever WrestleMania held?

    a. Staples Center
    b. M.G.M. Grand
    c. Maddison Square Garden
    d. 02 Arena

17. Who is credited for coming up with the name "WrestleMania"?

    a. Jerry Lawler
    b. Vince McMahon
    c. Howard Finkel
    d. Hulk Hogan

18. Which WWE executive conceptualized WrestleMania?

    a. Stephanie McMahon
    b. Triple H
    c. Vince McMahon
    d. Shane McMahon

19. What is the name of the WrestleMania event first organized with the Trump Organization?

a. WrestleMania Access

b. WrestleMania All Access

c. WrestleMania Axxess

d. WrestleMania Fest

20. Which superstar's career came to an end after a match against The Undertaker at WrestleMania XXVI?

a. Triple H

b. Shawn Michaels

c. Kane

d. The Big Show

21. Hulk Hogan won the first-ever main event at WrestleMania. Who was his opponent?

a. Mr. T

b. André the Giant

c. Stone Cold Steve Austin

d. Bret "The Hitman" Hart

22. Who has the record for beating the same superstar the most at WrestleMania?

a. Undertaker beating Triple H

b. Stone Cold Steve Austin beating The Rock

c. Shawn Michaels beating Bret "The Hitman" Hart

d. Triple H beating Kane

23. Which of these superstars served as a guest referee during a WrestleMania XX match between Goldberg and Brock Lesnar?

a. Shawn Michaels

b. Triple H

c. Vince McMahon

d. Stone Cold Steve Austin

24. Which of these WWE superstars ended "The Undertaker's" winning streak at WrestleMania?

    a. Triple H
    b. Kane
    c. Brock Lesnar
    d. Shawn Michaels

25. Which of these WWE superstars had his hair shaved by Donald Trump at WrestleMania?

    a. Bobby Lashley
    b. Vince McMahon
    c. Goldberg
    d. The Big Show

26. Which WWE legend delivered the infamous line "I'm sorry, I love you" before defeating Ric Flair to end his WWE career?

    a. Batista
    b. Randy Orton
    c. Shawn Michaels
    d. Triple H

27. Which of these boxers did Shawn Michaels get knocked out by at WrestleMania?

    a. Floyd Mayweather
    b. Mike Tyson
    c. Tyson Fury
    d. Muhammad Ali

28. Which WrestleMania marked the beginning of the "Austin Era"?

    a. WrestleMania X
    b. WrestleMania XI
    c. WrestleMania XIII
    d. WrestleMania XIV

29. Which of these superstars inflicted a body slam on André the Giant at WrestleMania III in what would be one of the most iconic WrestleMania moments?

    a. Hulk Hogan
    b. Ultimate Warrior
    c. Bret "The Hitman" Hart
    d. Stone Cold Steve Austin

ANSWERS

1. D – 1985

2. True

3. C – The Undertaker

4. B – Muhammad Ali

5. A – Triple H

6. B – The Undertaker

7. D – 36

8. A – Randy Savage

9. A – Hulk Hogan

10. B - Bret "The Hitman" Hart vs. Shawn Michaels

11. B – One Hour

12. B – The Undertaker

13. C – Mike Tyson

14. C – April

15. True

16. Madison Square Garden

17. C – Howard Finkel

18. C - Vince McMahon

19. C - WrestleMania Axxess

20. B – Shawn Michaels

21. A – Mr. T

22. A – The Undertaker beat Triple H

23. D - Stone Cold Steve Austin

24. C – Brock Lesnar

25. B – Vince McMahon

26. C – Shawn Michaels

27. B – Mike Tyson

28. D – WrestleMania XIV

29. A – Hulk Hogan

DID YOU KNOW?

- WrestleMania 2019 was the first to have a women's match as the main event.

- WrestleMania 32 had the most people in attendance in WrestleMania history. 101,763 people were in attendance.

CHAPTER 7:

INTERESTING FACTS ABOUT WWE (YOU PROBABLY WON'T BELIEVE)

TRIVIA TIME

1. Which of these legendary superstars never won a single title?

    a. Ultimate Warrior
    b. Chris Benoit
    c. Randy Savage
    d. Jake "The Snake" Roberts

2. Which of these former German National football team members became a WWE wrestler?

    a. Tim Weise
    b. Franz Beckenbauer
    c. Jurgen Klinsman
    d. Joachim Low

3. Which of these WWE superstars once fell asleep while competing in a match against John Stud?

    a. Hulk Hogan

b. Bruno Sammartino

c. Stone Cold Steve Austin

d. André the Giant

4. Which of these superstars initially used CM Punk's "Fire Burns" theme music?

   a. Kane

   b. John Cena

   c. Randy Orton

   d. Edge

5. True or False: Edge and Christian began their time in the WWE playing the role of brothers.

6. Which of these superstars won a title at age nineteen, making him the youngest ever champion?

   a. John Cena

   b. Xavier Woods

   c. Renee Dupree

   d. Randy Orton

7. Which WrestleMania event did not feature any men's singles match?

   a. WrestleMania 2

   b. WrestleMania IX

   c. WrestleMania XVI

   d. WrestleMania VII

8. Which of these WWE superstars was formerly a basketball player in Texas?

   a. The Undertaker

b. The Great Khali

c. Triple H

d. Titus O'Neil

9. A match between these two superstars is the only match to close a pay-per-view (breaking point 2009) and open the next one (Hell in a Cell)?

a. Kane vs. Triple H

b. The Undertaker vs. CM Punk

c. The Big Show vs. Mark Henry

d. Shawn Michaels vs. Randy Orton

10. All except one of these wrestlers are among the only five to have won five separate titles.

a. Kurt Angle

b. Jeff Hardy

c. Randy Orton

d. Chris Jericho

11. Which superstar featured on the cover of the first-ever *WWE* magazine?

a. Randy Savage

b. Owen Hart

c. Carlito

d. Vader

12. True or False: No title in WWE history has changed hands more times than the WWE Tag Team Championship.

13. Which of these WWE superstars has spent the most time in the ring?

    a. Randy Orton
    b. Rey Mysterio
    c. John Cena
    d. CM Punk

14. Which WWE superstar has forfeited the most titles?

    a. Triple H
    b. Brock Lesnar
    c. John Cena
    d. Shawn Michaels

15. Which of these superstars fought against members of the Evolution in three "unforgiven" pay-per-view events in three different years?

    a. Edge
    b. Mr. Kennedy
    c. Carlito
    d. Rob Van Dam

16. Which of these superstars never competed at any SummerSlam?

    a. Darren Young
    b. Christian
    c. Roddy Piper
    d. Stone Cold Steve Austin

17. Which two superstars were the first to feature using their real names in a WrestleMania main event?

    a. John Cena vs. Randy Orton

    b. Brock Lesnar vs. Kurt Angle

    c. Shane McMahon vs. Shawn Michaels

    d. Vince McMahon vs. Ric Flair

18. True or False: From 2005 to 2010, the last superstar to be eliminated in a Royal Rumble match ended up winning the World Title match at WrestleMania.

19. Three different superstars have won Royal Rumble matches, entering immediately after which superstar?

    a. Triple H

    b. Kurt Angle

    c. Kane

    d. The Undertaker

20. Which of these two superstars was involved in a personal brawl about protein shakes?

    a. Randy Orton and John Cena

    b. Sincara and Alberto Del Rio

    c. Yoshi Tatsu and Sheamus

    d. Bobby Lashley and Eric Rowen

ANSWERS

1. D - Jake "The Snake" Roberts

2. A - Tim Weise

3. D - André the Giant

4. C - Randy Orton

5. True

6. C - René Duprée

7. C - WrestleMania XVI

8. A - The Undertaker

9. B - The Undertaker vs. CM Punk

10. C - Randy Orton

11. D - Vader

12. True

13. B - Rey Mysterio

14. D - Shawn Michaels

15. C - Carlito

16. C - Roddy Piper

17. B - Brock Lesnar vs. Kurt Angle

18. False, but the last superstars to be eliminated between that time frame were all involved in WrestleMania World Title matches

19. A - Triple H

20. C - Yoshi Tatsu and Sheamus

DID YOU KNOW?

- At the end of WWE's 1999 *Backlash*, "The Undertaker" kidnapped Stephanie McMahon, which led to him holding a "Dark Wedding" on the *Monday Night Raw* following *Backlash*.

- In 2003, "The Big Show" returned to the ring after defeating "Rey Mysterio Jr" (after he was already placed on a stretcher), lifted him into the air and swung him like a baseball bat.

CHAPTER 8:

SPECIAL GUEST APPEARANCES

TRIVIA TIME

1. Which former American president has made multiple appearances on WWE?

   a. George Bush
   b. Barack Obama
   c. Bill Clinton
   d. Donald Trump

2. Which popular American actor got inducted into the WWE Hall of Fame in 2015?

   a. Gary Oldman
   b. Hugh Jackman
   c. John Goodman
   d. Arnold Schwarzenegger

3. Which English footballer was involved in a clash with "Bad News" Barrett on Raw in Manchester?

   a. David Beckham
   b. Wayne Rooney
   c. Steven Gerrard
   d. Frank Lampard

4. Which famous boxer was involved in a WrestleMania match vs. the "Big Show" in 2008?

    a. Floyd Mayweather
    b. Mike Tyson
    c. Anthony Joshua
    d. Tyson Fury

5. Which NBA Star served as an enforcer in a match between Chris Jericho and the "Big Show" on Raw?

    a. Michael Jordan
    b. Shaquille O'Neal
    c. Magic Johnson
    d. Lebron James

6. Which American actor was a guest on Monday Night Raw via Skype in 2012?

    a. Ashton Kutcher
    b. Neil Patrick Harris
    c. Charlie Sheen
    d. Joseph Gordon Lewitt

7. Which of these reality TV stars had a match at WrestleMania (and won)?

    a. Kim Kardashian
    b. Coco
    c. Paris Hilton
    d. Snooki

8. Which of these Civil Rights activists made an appearance as a guest host on Monday Night Raw to discuss

education reforms?

    a. The Rev. Al Sharpton

    b. Oprah Winfrey

    c. Louis Farrakhan

    d. John Lewis

9. Which popular comedy actor featured as a guest host on Monday Night Raw but only appeared backstage and never performed for the crowd in 2010?

    a. Charlie Sheen

    b. Ashton Kutcher

    c. Adam Sandler

    d. Ben Stiller

10. Which two actors appeared on Raw as hosts to promote their film *The Goods: Live Hard, Sell Hard*?

    a. Kevin James and Adam Sandler

    b. Jeremy Piven and Ken Jeong

    c. Mark Wahlberg and Will Ferrel

    d. Zach Galifianakis and Bradley Cooper

11. Which NASCAR driver is infamously known for calling Koffi Kingston, "Koff Johnston" while hosting Monday Night Raw?

    a. Joey Logano

    b. Denny Hamlin

    c. Kyle Busch

    d. Erik Jones

12. Who was the first guest star on Monday Night Raw?

    a. Batista

b. Beyoncé

c. Donald Trump

d. Taylor Lautner

13. Which billionaire rapper has made a WWE appearance?

a. Sean "Jay Z" Carter

b. Sean "Diddy" Combs

c. Dr. Dre

d. Kanye West

14. Which of these African American comedians made an appearance on Raw in September 2009?

a. Will Smith

b. Martin Lawrence

c. Bernie Mac

d. Cedric The Entertainer

15. Which famous American talk show host made an appearance on Raw in February 2015?

a. David Letterman

b. James Corden

c. Jerry Springer

d. Jimmy Kimmel

16. In 2011 Pitbull made an appearance as a guest on Raw. Which of the following women accompanied him?

a. Jennifer Lopez

b. Mýa

c. Selena Gomez

d. Shakira

17. This famous American singer has made guest

appearances in two different WWE decades.

   a. Dolly Parton
   b. Cyndi Lauper
   c. Aretha Franklin
   d. Celine Dion

18. Which of these Los Angeles rappers was featured as a guest on WWE?

   a. Kendrick Lamar
   b. 2pac Shakur
   c. Snoop Dogg
   d. Ice Cube

19. True or False: The only people to appear as guests on WWE Raw in 2019 are Michael Che and Colin Jost.

20. Which of these WWE superstars appeared on Raw playing the role of Santa Claus?

   a. The Undertaker
   b. Kane
   c. Mick Foley
   d. The Big Show

21. Which of these Marvel actors has appeared on WWE Raw as a guest host?

   a. Tom Holland
   b. Robert Downey Junior
   c. Bradley Cooper
   d. Paul Rudd

22. There has only been one guest appearance at 02 Arena. Who hosted?

a. David Hasselhoff
b. Michael Caine
c. Jay Cera
d. Seth Rogen

ANSWERS

1. D – Donald Trump

2. D – Arnold Schwarzenegger

3. B – Wayne Rooney

4. A – Floyd Mayweather

5. B – Shaquille O'Neal

6. C – Charlie Sheen

7. D – Snooki

8. A – The Rev. Al Sharpton

9. B – Ashton Kutcher

10. B - Jeremy Piven and Ken Jeong

11. C – Kyle Busch

12. A – Batista

13. B – Sean Diddy Combs

14. D – Cedric the Entertainer

15. B- Jerry Springer

16. B – Mýa

17. B – Cyndi Lauper

18. C – Snoop Dogg

19. True

20. C – Mick Foley

21. C – Bradley Cooper

22. A – David Hasselhoff

DID YOU KNOW?

- WrestleMania is one short of having one hundred celebrity involvements over the span of their events.

- WWE Raw has featured a total of ninety-two stars in seventy-three episodes.

- Since the 1980s, celebrity guest appearances have become a mainstay in WWE. Actors, musicians, and sports stars have made frequent appearances on their various shows.

- Donald Trump introduced the concept of having celebrities on Monday Night Raw. He, at the time, was involved heavily in Raw operations.

- Some retired WWE stars return as celebrity guest stars.

CHAPTER 9:

WWE RAW

TRIVIA TIME

1. In what year did WWE Raw premiere?

    a. 1991
    b. 1992
    c. 1993
    d. 1994

2. How many nations have hosted Live broadcasts of WWE Raw?

    a. Ten
    b. Nine
    c. Eight
    d. Seven

3. WWE Raw is a(an) _____ show?

    a. Annual
    b. Daily
    c. Weekly
    d. Monthly

4. True or False: The first-ever WWE Heavyweight Champion was signed to the WWE Raw roster.

5. True or False: WWE Raw is the longest-running weekly episodic show in the United States history.

6. In 2019, WWE Raw got nominated for the TV Show of the Year award. Did they receive the award?

   a. Yes
   b. No
   c. Yes, but it was shared

7. Which African country has hosted a Live broadcast of WWE Raw?

   a. Nigeria
   b. Ghana
   c. Sierra Leone
   d. South Africa

8. What color serves as the signature color for WWE Raw?

   a. Red
   b. Blue
   c. Green
   d. Black

9. Which WWE superstar died during an in-ring stunt during a recording of an episode of WWE Raw?

   a. Eddie Guerrero
   b. Chris Benoit
   c. Owen Hart
   d. André the Giant

10. Which WWE superstar has the most wins on WWE Raw?

a. Edge
b. Kane
c. John Cena
d. Ric Flair

11. On what day of the week do episodes of WWE Raw air?

    a. Monday
    b. Friday
    c. Sunday
    d. Saturday

12. On which of these famous American networks did WWE Raw premiere?

    a. TNN
    b. The USA Network
    c. Spike TV
    d. ESPN

13. True or False: The early episodes of WWE Raw were recorded on the seventh floor of the Manhattan Center in New York City.

14. The highest-rated Monday Night Raw episode took place on May 10th, 1999, and featured a tag team match between?

    a. Edge, Christian and Chris Jericho vs. Ric Flair, Triple H and Batista
    b. Vince McMahon, The Rock, and Stone Cold Steve Austin vs. Shane McMahon, Triple H, and The Undertaker
    c. The Miz, John Morrisson, and Daniel Bryan vs.

Bobby Lashley, Antonio Cesaro, and Sheamus

d. Rey Mysterio, Eddie Guerrero and Chavo Guerrero vs. John Cena, Randy Orton, and Edge

15. The highest-rated segment on WWE Monday Night Raw was hosted by which of these superstars?

   a. The Miz
   b. Kevin Owens
   c. Stone Cold Steve Austin
   d. Mick Foley

16. The Kings Court was a special segment on Raw hosted by?

   a. King Booker
   b. Triple H (The King of Kings)
   c. Jerry "The King" Lawler
   d. Vince McMahon

17. True or False: Raw had a special segment known as WWE Diva Search.

18. What was the name of the show hosted by Carlito on Raw?

   a. Carlito's Way
   b. Carlito's Cabal
   c. Carlito's Cabana
   d. Carlito's House

19. The Master Lock challenge was a recurring segment between 2005 and 2007 hosted by which of these superstars?

a. Kurt Angle
b. Chris Masters
c. John Cena
d. Edge

20. The VIP lounge was a segment hosted by which of these superstars?

a. R-Truth
b. Kevin Owens
c. M.V.P.
d. The Miz

21. What was the name of the show hosted by Shawn Michaels?

a. The Heartbreak Hotel
b. The Heartbreak Show
c. The Heartbreak Kid
d. The Heartbreak Live

22. True or False: The Love Shack was a segment hosted by Dude Love between 1997 and 1998.

23. Which of these superstars hosted the segment known as "The Highlights Reel"?

a. Edge
b. Christian
c. Chris Jericho
d. Randy Savage

24. Which of these superstars hosted the segment "White Boy Challenge"?

a. Goldberg
b. Brock Lesnar
c. Edge
d. Rodney Mack

25. The Kiss Cam segment on Raw was hosted by which WWE diva?

a. Katilyn
b. Maria
c. Natalya
d. AJ Lee

26. Who was the first-ever general manager of Raw?

a. Vince McMahon
b. Eric Bischoff
c. William Regal
d. Mick Foley

27. Which of these pairings served as the first-ever commentators on WWE Raw?

a. Vince McMahon and Johnny Polo
b. Gorilla Monsoon and Shawn Michaels
c. Randy Savage and Vince McMahon
d. Jerry Lawler and Michael Cole

28. WWE AM Raw was a show that aired on which days of the week?

a. Monday night and Tuesday morning
b. Saturday night and Sunday morning
c. Friday night and Saturday morning
d. Wednesday morning and Thursday morning

29. Which of these superstars defeated Koko B. Ware to win the first-ever match on Raw?

    a. Mr. Fuji
    b. Yokozuna
    c. Rikishi
    d. Shawn Michaels

30. Which of these superstars won against Max Moon to become the first-ever superstar to retain a title (WWF Intercontinental Championship) on the first episode of Raw?

    a. The Undertaker
    b. Triple H
    c. Shawn Michaels
    d. Stone Cold Steve Austin

ANSWERS

1. C – 1993

2. A – Ten

3. C – Weekly

4. True

5. True

6. B - No

7. D – South Africa

8. A – Red

9. C – Owen Hart

10. B – Kane

11. A – Monday

12. B - The USA Network

13. True

14. B - Vince McMahon, The Rock, and Stone Cold Steve Austin vs. Shane McMahon, Triple H, and The Undertaker

15. D – Mick Foley

16. C – Jerry "The King" Lawler

17. True

18. C – Carlito's Cabana

19. B – Chris Masters

20. C – MVP

21. A – The Heartbreak Hotel

22. True

23. C – Chris Jericho

24. D – Rodney Mack

25. B – Maria

26. B – Eric Bischoff

27. C - Randy Savage and Vince McMahon

28. B – Saturday Nights and Sunday Morning

29. B – Yokozuna

30. C – Shawn Michaels

DID YOU KNOW?

- WWE Raw was initially supposed to be called "Uncooked Raw." The name was suggested by former Vice President of Business Operations Dick Glover before it was shortened.

- The show currently airs every Monday at 8 pm EST.

- WWE Raw has had over six million attendees in its history.

- Raw has been broadcast Live from 208 different arenas.

- WWE Raw is also known as Monday Night Raw or Raw.

- Monday Night Wars was a term coined when WWE (WWF at the time) Monday Night Raw went head-to-head in a rating war between the brand and Monday Nitro, a show by their fierce competitors, WCW.

CHAPTER 10:

WWE SMACKDOWN!

TRIVIA TIME

1. On what day of the week does WWE SmackDown air?
    a. Monday
    b. Tuesday
    c. Thursday
    d. Friday

2. On what network does WWE SmackDown currently air?
    a. Netflix
    b. Fox
    c. Hulu
    d. Amazon Prime

3. In what year did the first episode of WWE SmackDown air?
    a. 1996
    b. 1997
    c. 1998
    d. 1999

4. On what network did WWE SmackDown initially air?

a. UPN
b. FX
c. The CW
d. TNT

5. The opening theme song of WWE SmackDown is a song by a famous rock and roll band. Which band is that?

a. Queen
b. AC/DC
c. Guns N Roses
d. The Beatles

6. WWE SmackDown has had special episodes in honor of all but one of these superstars.

a. John Cena
b. Vince McMahon
c. The Rock
d. The Undertaker

7. True or False: Ed Koskey is the creator of WWE SmackDown.

8. WWE SmackDown has aired in how many countries?

a. Three
b. Five
c. Seven
d. Nine

9. WWE SmackDown held a special episode called "A Tribute to the Troops." Where was the Live broadcast

held?

a. The United States of America
b. Vietnam
c. Iraq
d. Israel

10. In what year did WWE SmackDown celebrate its 1,000th episode?

a. 2016
b. 2017
c. 2018
d. 2019

11. All but one of these individuals serve as producers of WWE SmackDown.

a. Triple H
b. Vince McMahon
c. Bruce Prichard
d. Kevin Dunne

12. WWE SmackDown has been aired on all of the following networks except?

a. Hulu
b. NBC Universal
c. The CW
d. Fox

13. Which famous superstar used the catchphrase "SmackDown" before the inception of WWE

SmackDown?

    a. Stone Cold Steve Austin
    b. The Rock
    c. Goldberg
    d. Vince McMahon

14. True or False: In 2008, WWE SmackDown aired on The CW.

15. Which of these women has served the most tenures as the general manager of SmackDown?

    a. Paige
    b. Vickie Guerrero
    c. Stephanie McMahon
    d. Ronda Rousey

16. True or False: Stephanie McMahon stepped down as the general manager of Smackdown after an "I quit" match.

17. Who has served the most years as general manager of Raw?

    a. Eric Bischoff
    b. Theodore Long
    c. Stephanie McMahon
    d. Vickie Guerrero

18. Which commentator pairing was the first-ever on SmackDown?

    a. Jim Ross and Jerry Lawler
    b. Jerry Lawler and Michael Cole

    c. Michael Cole and Jim Cornette

    d. Tazz and Mick Foley

19. In what year did Miz start his segment, "Miz TV"?

    a. 2010

    b. 2011

    c. 2012

    d. 2013

20. Which of these superstars hosted "The Peep Show" on SmackDown?

    a. Chris Jericho

    b. Christian

    c. Edge

    d. Shawn Michaels

21. Which of these people has served as both the General Manager and a commentator of SmackDown?

    a. John Bradshaw Layfield

    b. Paul Heyman

    c. Triple H

    d. David Otunga

22. True or False: The segment known as Carlito's Cabana was originally on SmackDown.

ANSWERS

1. D - Friday

2. B – Fox

3. D – 1999

4. A - UPN

5. B – AC/DC

6. B – Vince McMahon

7. False – Ed Koskey is only a lead writer for WWE SmackDown

8. C – Seven

9. C – Iraq

10. C – 2018

11. A - Triple H

12. A – Hulu

13. B – The Rock

14. False

DID YOU KNOW?

- WWE SmackDown was created to be a direct competitor to WCW's Thursday Night SmackDown.

- WWE SmackDown has never held a Live broadcast on African soil.

- WWE SmackDown is one of the two flagship shows of WWE.

- All archived episodes of the WWE SmackDown weekly show were made available on the WWE network in 2017.

- WWE SmackDown was initially billed to be an all-women affair, but there wasn't enough talent for it.

- Since its inception, WWE SmackDown has had a PG rating. The only WWE show with that rating.

CHAPTER 11:

WWE HALL OF FAME

TRIVIA TIME

1. Who was the first-ever WWE Hall Of Fame Inductee?

    a. Hulk Hogan
    b. André the Giant
    c. Bret "The Hitman" Hart
    d. Owen Hart

2. Which of these superstars was inducted into the WWE Hall of Fame by Vince McMahon?

    a. James Dudley
    b. Gorilla Monsoon
    c. Chief Jay Strongbow
    d. Arnold Skaaland

3. True or False: Ric Flair and Shawn Michaels are the only two superstars with double Hall of Fame inductions.

4. One of these four superstars was not inducted while still being an active member of the WWE.

    a. Jeff Jarett
    b. Shawn Michaels

    c. Triple H

    d. Kurt Angle

5. **True or False**: There have been fewer than forty posthumous WWE Hall of Fame inductees.

6. Which of these groups has received Hall of Fame inductions?

    a. The Four Horsemen

    b. The New Day

    c. The Usos

    d. S.H.I.E.L.D

7. **True or False**: There have been at least ten celebrity WWE Hall of Fame inductions.

8. **Which** of these superstars inducted Ric Flair into the WWE Hall of Fame in 2008?

    a. Shawn Michaels

    b. Shane McMahon

    c. Dave Batista

    d. Triple H

9. Hulk Hogan's Hall of Fame induction was done by which of these popular actors?

    a. Sylvester Stallone

    b. Arnold Schwarzenegger

    c. Robert De Niro

    d. Jo Pesci

10. True Or False: Stone Cold Steve Austin is a WWE Hall of Fame inductee.

11. True or False: There have been over 110 wrestlers inducted into the WWE Hall of Fame.

12. How many warrior award recipients have there been?

    a. Three
    b. Four
    c. Five
    d. Six

13. **True or False**: There have been up to fifteen groups inducted into the WWE Hall of Fame.

14. Which of these WWE Legends did Cody and Dustin Rhodes induct into the WWE Hall of Fame?

    a. Bret "The Hitman" Hart
    b. Vince McMahon
    c. Batista
    d. Dusty Rhodes

15. In what year did Ted Dibiase get inducted into the Hall of Fame?

    a. 2010
    b. 2011
    c. 2012
    d. 2013

16. Which of these people were not inducted into the Hall of Fame in 2007?

    a. Jerry "The King" Lawler
    b. Mr. Fuji
    c. Jim Ross

d. Yokozuna

17. The Dudley Boyz were inducted into the WWE Hall of Fame by which former WWE Tag Team champions?

    a. Triple H and Shawn Michaels
    b. The Usos
    c. Edge and Christian
    d. Kane and The Undertaker

18. The late Eddie Guerrero was represented by which of these superstars on the day of his induction?

    a. Chavo Guerrero
    b. Chris Benoit
    c. Rey Mysterio
    d. Vickie Guerrero

19. Which of these rappers has been inducted into the WWE Hall of Fame?

    a. Eminem
    b. Diddy
    c. Snoop Dogg
    d. Dr. Dre

20. Goldberg's Hall of Fame induction was announced by?

    a. Jim Ross
    b. Jerry "The King" Lawler
    c. Michael Cole
    d. Paul Heyman

21. Which of these individuals received the first Ultimate Warrior award?

a. Joan Lunden
b. Jarius "J.J." Robertson
c. Connor Michalek
d. Eric LeGrand

22. True or False: The Bella twins were the only inductees into the WWE Hall of Fame in 2020.

23. Mark Henry's Hall of Fame induction was announced by which of these WWE superstars?

a. Kane
b. Titus O'Neil
c. The Big Show
d. Umaga

24. WWE Diva Natalya announced the induction of which of these legends?

a. Paige
b. Beth Phoenix
c. Charlotte Flair
d. Michelle McCool

25. Which of these boxers is a Hall of Fame inductee?

a. Floyd Mayweather
b. Mike Tyson
c. Tyson Fury
d. Anthony Joshua

26. True or False: "Cowboy" Bob Orton was inducted into the Hall of Fame by his son Randy Orton.

27. In what year was the first WWE Hall of Famer

announced?

    a. 1991

    b. 1992

    c. 1993

    d. 1994

28. Who was the first WWE Hall of Fame inductee?

    a. André the Giant

    b. Hulk Hogan

    c. Ultimate Warrior

    d. Bret "The Hitman" Hart

29. Roddy Piper was inducted into the Hall of Fame by whom?

    a. Triple H

    b. Edge

    c. Shawn Michaels

    d. Ric Flair

ANSWERS

1. B – André the Giant

2. A – James Dudley

3. True

4. B – Shawn Michaels

5. False

6. A – The Four Horsemen

7. True

8. Triple H

9. A – Sylvester Stallone

10. True

11. True

12. C – Five

13. True

14. D – Dusty Rhodes

15. A – 2010

16. D – Yokozuna P

17. C – Edge and Christian

18. D – Vickie Guerrero

19. C - Snoop Dogg

20. D - Paul Heyman

21. C - Connor Michalek

22. False

23. C - The Big Show

24. B - Beth Phoenix

25. B - Mike Tyson

26. True

27. C - 1993

28. A - André the Giant

29. C - Ric Flair

CHAPTER 12:

WWE COUPLES

TRIVIA TIME

1. Sharmell Sullivan-Huffman was the on-screen manager of which of these superstars who later became her husband in 2005?

   a. R-Truth
   b. Booker T
   c. Sheamus
   d. Seth Rollins

2. Which WWE couple had their wedding air on the Total Bellas TV show?

   a. Brie Bella and Daniel Bryan
   b. AJ Lee and Daniel Bryan
   c. Becky Lynch and Seth Rollins
   d. Seth Rollins and Nikki Bella

3. In 2003, Stephanie McMahon got married to which of these Superstars?

   a. Shawn Michaels
   b. Batista
   c. Triple H
   d. Shane McMahon

4. Former WWF women's champion, Sable, is married to which of these former WWE World Heavyweight champions?

    a. The Undertaker
    b. Brock Lesnar
    c. Stone Cold Steve Austin
    d. Edge

5. The Undertaker got married to a former two-time WWE Divas champion in 2010. Who is she?

    a. Ronda Rousey
    b. Charlotte Flair
    c. Michelle McCool
    d. Asuka

6. WWE Diva AJ Lee is currently married to which of these former WWE superstars?

    a. The Rock
    b. Dean Ambrose
    c. Luke Harper
    d. CM Punk

7. WWE Diva Naomi is married to one of the U.S.O. brothers. Which one of them?

    a. Jimmy
    b. Jay

8. True or False: Vickie Guerrero was married to the late WWE legend Eddie Guerrero.

9. Reby Sky is married to one of the Hardy brothers.

Which one of them?

   a. Matt

   b. Jeff

10. Chelsea Green tied the knot with one of these superstars.

   a. Dolph Ziggler

   b. Zack Ryder

   c. Alberto Del Rio

   d. Big E Langston

11. The wedding of the Miz and Maryse took place in what year?

   a. 2013

   b. 2014

   c. 2015

   d. 2016

12. Rusev and Lana were a match made by which WWE legend?

   a. Dusty Rhodes

   b. Hulk Hogan

   c. Stone Cold Steve Austin

   d. Goldberg

13. Natalya got married to a long-time sweetheart and friend of the family. Who is the superstar?

   a. Tyson Kidd

   b. Cody Rhodes

   c. Christian

d. Bobby Lashley

14. Former S.H.I.E.L.D member Dean Ambrose is married to which of these WWE Divas?

    a. Charlotte Flair
    b. Renee Young
    c. Natalya
    d. Naya Jax

15. The daughter of WWE legend Ric Flair and WWE Diva Charlotte Flair is married to which WWE superstar?

    a. Andrade
    b. Dean Ambrose
    c. Seth Rollins
    d. Roman Reigns

16. Becky Lynch is currently engaged to which of these WWE superstars?

    a. Seth Rollins
    b. John Cena
    c. Randy Orton
    d. Goldberg

ANSWERS

1. B – Booker T

2. A - Brie Bella and Daniel Bryan

3. C – Triple H

4. B – Brock Lesnar

5. C – Michelle McCool

6. D – CM Punk

7. A - Jimmy

8. A – Matt

9. B – Zack Ryder

10. B – 2014

11. A – Dusty Rhodes

12. A – Tyson Kidd

13. B – Renee Young

14. A – Andrade

15. A – Seth Rollins

DID YOU KNOW?

- Nikki Bella and John Cena were to be married, but the relationship came to an end, much to WWE fans' displeasure. The Diva had been married before him.

CHAPTER 13:

WWE NXT

TRIVIA TIME

1. In what year did the first episode of WWE NXT air?

    a. 2010
    b. 2011
    c. 2012
    d. 2013

2. Which WWE superstar was the inaugural winner of the NXT show, and who mentored him?

    a. Finn Balor mentored by John Cena
    b. Titus O'Neil mentored by Bobby Lashley
    c. Wade Barett mentored by Chris Jericho
    d. Johnny Curtis mentored by Shawn Michaels

3. How many winners of NXT Champions have there been so far?

    a. Eighteen
    b. Ten
    c. Five
    d. Six

4. Which of these WWE superstars has the most NXT match wins?

a. Roman Reigns
b. The Fiend
c. Drew McIntyre
d. Asuka

5. Which of these WWE super groups began at NXT?

a. S.H.I.E.L.D
b. Evolution
c. D Generation X
d. Hardy Boys

6. Which tag-team is the longest-reigning in NXT history?

a. The Hype Bros
b. The Lucha Dragos
c. The Ascension
d. The American Alpha

7. Who is the first-ever NXT champion?

a. Seth Rollins
b. Roman Reigns
c. Wade Barrett
d. Dean Ambrose

8. True or False: Dean Ambrose is the only member of the S.H.I.E.L.D that did not debut on NXT.

9. Which of these former NXT stars is not currently under contract in the WWE?

a. Big E Langston
b. Roman Reigns
c. Adam Rose

    d. Jinda Mahal

10. True or False: The NXT has the most title changes for any WWE men's singles championship.

11. Which of these superstars served as the first host of NXT?

    a. Wade Barrett
    b. William Regal
    c. Matt Striker
    d. Dusty Rhodes

12. Which superstar served as the first commissioner of the NXT?

    a. Dusty Rhodes
    b. John Bradshaw Layfield
    c. William Regal
    d. Jeff Jarrett

13. Who was the first general manager of NXT?

    a. Michael Cole
    b. Jerry Lawler
    c. William Regal
    d. Wade Barrett

ANSWERS

1. A – 2010

2. C - Wade Barett mentored by Chris Jericho

3. A – Eighteen

4. D – Asuka

5. A – S.H.I.E.L.D

6. C – The Ascension

7. A - Seth Rollins

8. True

9. C – Adam Rose

10. True

11. C – Matt Striker

12. A – Dusty Rodes

13. C – William Regal

DID YOU KNOW?

- There have only been two superstars (Brock Lesnar and Goldberg) who have been WWE universal champions that never had a stint on the NXT.

- NXT was created to be a development brand for WWE, with the best stars being promoted to the main roster.

CHAPTER 14:

WWE DIVAS

TRIVIA TIME

1. Which WWE Diva holds the record for most combined days as Divas champion?

    a. AJ Lee
    b. Brie Bella
    c. Nia Jax
    d. Natalya

2. Which WWE Diva holds the record for longest individual reign as Divas champion?

    a. Brie Bella
    b. Nikki Bella
    c. Eve Torres
    d. Michelle McCool

3. Which WWE Diva has the most reigns as joint WWE divas champ with AJ Lee?

    a. Becky Lynch
    b. Charlotte Flair
    c. Eve Torres
    d. Natalya

4. Jillian Hall holds the record for the shortest reign. How long did it last?

    a. Five minutes
    b. Ten minutes
    c. Two minutes
    d. One minute

5. When was the WWE Divas Championship created?

    a. 2006
    b. 2007
    c. 2008
    d. 2009

6. Which WWE Diva became the inaugural Divas Championship?

    a. Michelle McCool
    b. Aj Lee
    c. Brie Bella
    d. Nikki Bella

7. **True or False:** Stephanie McMahon conceptualized the title.

8. Who is the oldest WWE Divas champion?

    a. Layla
    b. Natalya
    c. Stephanie McMahon
    d. Nia Jax

9. Who is the youngest WWE Divas champion?

    a. AJ Lee

b. Paige

c. Charlotte Flair

d. Asuka

10. What is the name of the TV show for the WWE female roster?

    a. WWE Divas

    b. Total Bellas

    c. Total Divas

    d. DivaMania

11. Which WWE Diva won the first-ever WWE Unified Divas Championship?

    a. Melina

    b. Michelle McCool

    c. Paige

    d. Katilyn

12. When were the WWE Women's Championship and WWE Divas Championship unified?

    a. 2009

    b. 2010

    c. 2011

    d. 2012

13. Which legendary female wrestler was the first to proclaim herself as a "diva"?

    a. Sunny

    b. Marlena

    c. Sable

d. Debra

14. In what year did the first-ever Divas main event of the W.W.F. between Stephanie McMahon and Lita occur?

    a. 1999
    b. 2000
    c. 2001
    d. 2002

15. What was the name of the reality show WWE organized as a platform for Divas to get signed to WWE?

    a. WWE Tough Enough
    b. WWE Strong Enough
    c. WWE Big Enough
    d. WWE She's Enough

16. Which of these Divas shortly held the male WWE Cruiserweight Championship in 2004?

    a. Candice Michelle
    b. Jacqueline
    c. Beth Phoenix
    d. Mickie James

17. Which WWE Diva became the first to hold the Divas Championship twice?

    a. Mickie James
    b. Sable
    c. Eve Torres
    d. Maryse

18. Which WWE Diva became the first NXT graduate to

win the WWE Divas Championship?

a. Katilyn
b. Eve Torres
c. Stephanie McMahon
d. AJ Lee

19. True or False: WrestleMania XXX was the first time the WWE Divas Championship would be defended at WrestleMania.

20. Who is the youngest Divas champion in WWE history?

a. AJ Lee
b. Paige
c. Trish
d. Stephanie McMahon

21. Which WWE Diva became the first to appear on the cover of Playboy magazine in 1999?

a. Chyna
b. Torrie Wilson
c. Christy Hemme
d. Sable

ANSWERS

1. A – AJ Lee

2. B – Nikki Bella

3. C – Eve Torres

4. B – Ten minutes

5. C – 2008

6. A – Michelle McCool

7. False

8. A – Layla

9. B – Paige

10. C – Total Divas

11. A – Melina

12. B – 2010

13. C - Sable

14. B - 2000

15. A - WWE tough enough

16. B - Jacqueline

17. D - Maryse

18. A - Katilyn

19. True

20. B - Paige

21. D - Sable

DID YOU KNOW?

- During WWE's pay-per-view, "The World's Greatest Royal Rumble" in Saudi Arabia, the Divas were not allowed to participate due to restrictions on how women could be portrayed in the Arab country. The Divas were adequately compensated for their absence.

- The Bella twins were both soccer players for Scottsdale Club in elementary school before becoming professional wrestlers.

CHAPTER 15:

PAY-PER-VIEW

TRIVIA TIME

1. Which of these is considered the second biggest WWE event of the year, after WrestleMania?

    a. Tables, Ladders, and Chairs (T.L.C.)
    b. Summerslam
    c. Royal Rumble
    d. Hell in a Cell

2. In what year did the Survivor Series commence?

    a. 1987
    b. 1988
    c. 1989
    d. 1990

3. Which of these is not among the "Big Four" PPV events of WWE

    a. SummerSlam
    b. Tables, Ladders, and Chairs (T.L.C.)
    c. WrestleMania
    d. Survivor Series

4. Which pay-per-view event involves superstars getting an opportunity to win a contract for a title shot?

a. King of the Ring
b. Tables, Ladders, and Chairs (T.L.C.)
c. Money in The Bank
d. Hell in a Cell

5. Which WWE pay-per-view event involves an André the Giant dedication match?

a. Royal Rumble
b. WrestleMania
c. Money in the Bank
d. Tables, Ladders, and Chairs (T.L.C.)

6. Which of these WWE events is headlined by steel cages?

a. Extreme Rules
b. Summerslam
c. Hell in a Hell
d. Survivor Series

7. Which WWE event involves a lack of set rules and guidelines?

a. Hell in a Cell
b. Tables, Ladders, and Chairs (T.L.C.)
c. Survivor Series
d. Extreme Rules

8. **True or False**: The WWE King of the Ring is awarded to the superstar who wins the Money in the Bank contract.

9. What is the longest-running WWE pay-per-view event?

a. King of the Ring
b. SummerSlam
c. WrestleMania
d. Royal Rumble

10. Which WWE pay-per-view has the longest run time?

    a. Summerslam
    b. WrestleMania
    c. Tables, Ladders, and Chairs (T.L.C.)
    d. Hell in a Cell

11. **True or False**: Money in the Bank is the WWE event dubbed "the biggest party of the summer."

12. In what year was the first-ever Royal Rumble event held?

    a. 1985
    b. 1986
    c. 1987
    d. 1988

13. Which pay-per-view event is mostly regarded as the most successful single pay-per-view event?

    a. SummerSlam 2010
    b. Royal Rumble 1990
    c. WrestleMania III
    d. WrestleMania I

14. Which pay-per-view event got added to the Big Four to make it the Classic Five?

    a. King of the Ring

b. Hell in a Cell
c. Tables, Ladders, and Chairs (T.L.C.)
d. Vengeance

ANSWERS

1. B – SummerSlam

2. A – 1987

3. B – Tables, Ladders, and Chairs (T.L.C.)

4. C – Money in the Bank

5. B – WrestleMania

6. C – Hell in A Cell

7. D – Extreme Rules

8. False

9. C – WrestleMania

10. B – WrestleMania

11. False – SummerSlam is referred to as the biggest party of the summer

12. D – 1988

13. C – WrestleMania III

14. A – King of The Ring

DID YOU KNOW?

- WrestleMania 28 is the highest-grossing WWE pay-per-view event of all time, grossing 1.25 million dollars. The main event was a "once in a lifetime" match between The Rock and John Cena, two of WWE's most electric superstars.

- With the rise of streaming, the dynamic of WWE pay-per-view events have changed. Viewers can now subscribe to the WWE network and not have to buy each PPV separately.

CHAPTER 16:

ROYAL RUMBLE

TRIVIA TIME

1. Which superstar has won the most Royal Rumble matches?
   a. Shawn Michaels
   b. Kane
   c. Stone Cold Steve Austin
   d. The Big Show

2. How many Royal Rumble events have there been in WWE history?
   a. 34
   b. 33
   c. 32
   d. 31

3. Who won the first-ever Royal Rumble event?
   a. Hulk Hogan
   b. Big John Studd
   c. Ric Flair
   d. Jim Duggan

4. How many female Royal Rumble matches have taken place at WWE Royal Rumble?

a. 2
b. 3
c. 4
d. 5

5. Which WWE Diva was the first to win a title Royal Rumble match?

   a. Charlotte Flair
   b. Asuka
   c. AJ Lee
   d. Bianca Belair

6. Which number is known as the "Lucky Royal Rumble Number" because most winners have been at that number?

   a. 30
   b. 1
   c. 27
   d. 24

7. Which WWE superstar has the most combined Royal Rumble eliminations?

   a. Kane
   b. Hulk Hogan
   c. Shawn Michaels
   d. Edge

8. Which superstar is tied with Brock Lesnar with the most eliminations in a single match?

a. The Big Show
b. Edge
c. Braun Strowman
d. John Cena

9. True or False: Vince McMahon and Randy Orton are the only two superstars to win with only one elimination.

10. Which WWE superstar has the longest cumulative Royal Rumble time?

a. Rey Mysterio
b. Triple H
c. Randy Orton
d. Chris Jericho

11. Which WWE Diva has the most combined eliminations at Royal Rumble?

a. Nia Jax
b. Bianca Belair
c. Shayna Baszler
d. Charlotte Flair

12. Which WWE superstar is the only person to win from the same slot twice?

a. Batista
b. Ric Flair
c. Stone Cold Steve Austin
d. Chris Jericho

13. Which WWE Diva has the joint-most eliminations in a single Royal Rumble match with Bianca Belair?

a. Shayna Baszler
b. Charlotte Flair
c. Nia Jax
d. Ronda Rousey

ANSWERS

1. B – Kane

2. D – 31

3. D – Jim Duggan

4. C – 4

5. B – Asuka

6. C – 27

7. A – Kane

8. C - Braun Strowman

9. True

10. D – Chris Jericho

11. C - Shayna Baszler

12. A – Batista

13. A - Shayna Baszler

DID YOU KNOW?

- Royal Rumble 2008 was the first WWE pay-per-view event to be broadcast in high definition.

- There have been draws in Royal Rumble matches happening when the feet of the final two superstars land on the floor at the same time.

- A rematch can be requested in situations where the officials could not ascertain whose leg landed outside first. An example of this was in a match where Batista and John Cena were the final two superstars.

CHAPTER 17:

SUMMERSLAM

TRIVIA TIME

1. In what year did the inaugural SummerSlam event take place?

   a. 1988
   b. 1989
   c. 1990
   d. 1991

2. Where was the venue of the first SummerSlam event?

   a. Staples Center
   b. 02 arena
   c. Madison Square Garden
   d. Copps Coliseum

3. Which of these superstars has the most wins at SummerSlam?

   a. The Undertaker
   b. Edge
   c. Shawn Michaels
   d. Randy Orton

4. Which of these superstars has competed in the most SummerSlam matches?

a. Stone Cold Steve Austin
b. Goldberg
c. The Undertaker
d. Hulk Hogan

5. True or False: Out of Hulk Hogan's six SummerSlam appearances, only three have been singles matches.

6. Which superstar holds the most extensive undefeated record at SummerSlam?

    a. The Undertaker
    b. Randy Orton
    c. John Cena
    d. Hulk Hogan

7. Razor Ramon was involved in a legendary ladder match against one of these superstars.

    a. Triple H
    b. Shawn Michaels
    c. Batista
    d. Hulk Hogan

8. Which of these superstars participated in the first five SummerSlams and won all his matches?

    a. Ultimate Warrior
    b. Bret "The Hitman" Hart
    c. Randy Savage
    d. Hulk Hogan

9. Which of these superstars has the longest SummerSlam career (twenty-one years)?

a. Hulk Hogan
b. Bret "The Hitman" Hart
c. John Cena
d. Ultimate Warrior

10. True or False: The longest singles match at SummerSlam took place between brothers Bret "The Hitman" Hart and Owen Hart.

11. Which of these superstars is the first and only superstar to face himself at SummerSlam?

    a. Kane
    b. The Undertaker
    c. Shawn Michaels
    d. The Big Show

12. Which of these superstars headlined the first-ever SummerSlam under the alias "The Super Powers"?

    a. Hulk Hogan and Randy Savage
    b. Ted Dibiase and André the Giant
    c. Bret "The Hitman" Hart and Ultimate Warrior
    d. Honky Tonk Man and Vince McMahon

13. Which of these superstars holds the record for the most consecutive years with matches at SummerSlam?

    a. Triple H
    b. Ric Flair
    c. Shawn Michaels
    d. The Undertaker

14. Which of these superstars has the most losses at SummerSlam?

a. The Undertaker
b. Triple H
c. Shawn Michaels
d. Ric Flair

15. True or False: The Undertaker has never successfully won or defended the World Heavyweight Championship or the WWE Championship at Summer-Slam.

16. How many superstars with five or more matches are undefeated at SummerSlam?

    a. One
    b. Two
    c. Three
    d. Four

17. True or False: Edge is a SummerSlam triple champion, having won or defended three different titles at SummerSlam.

18. Kurt Angles's only SummerSlam loss came in a triple threat match between him and which two other superstars?

    a. Triple H and Shawn Michaels
    b. Goldberg and Stone Cold Steve Austin
    c. Vince McMahon and Shane McMahon
    d. The Rock and Triple H

19. Which of these superstars did Triple H face in an unsolicited street fight at SummerSlam 2002?

a. Kurt Angle
b. Kevin Nash
c. The Rock
d. Shawn Michaels

ANSWERS

1. A - 1988

2. C - Madison Square Garden

3. A – The Undertaker

4. C - The Undertaker

5. True

6. D – Hulk Hogan

7. B - Shawn Michaels

8. A - Ultimate Warrior

9. B - Bret "The Hitman" Hart

10. True

11. B - The Undertaker

12. A - Hulk Hogan and Randy Savage

13. D - The Undertaker

14. A - The Undertaker

15. True

16. B - Two

17. True

18. D - The Rock and Triple H

19. D - Shawn Michaels

CHAPTER 18:

KING OF THE RING

TRIVIA TIME

1. When was the first-ever King of the Ring tournament?

    a. 1984
    b. 1985
    c. 1986
    d. 1987

2. In what year did the King of the Ring tournament become a pay-per-view event?

    a. 1991
    b. 1992
    c. 1993
    d. 1994

3. Who won the first-ever King of the Ring tournament?

    a. Bruno Sammartino
    b. André the Giant
    c. Don Muraco
    d. Hulk Hogan

4. Which King played the King of the Ring into his "King of Wrestling" gimmick?

a. Don Muraco

b. Harley Race

c. Hulk Hogan

d. Bruno Sammartino

5. Which King of the Ring was known as the "King of Harts?"

a. Owen Hart

b. Bret "The Hitman" Hart

c. Randy Savage

d. Shawn Michaels

6. When Edge was King of the Ring, he was also known as?

a. The Great

b. The Mighty

c. The Awesome

d. The Ruthless

7. Which King of the Ring was also known as "The Macho King"?

a. Ultimate Warrior

b. Randy Savage

c. Triple H

d. Hulk Hogan

8. True or False: Stone Cold Steve Austin's Austin 3:16 started at the King of the Ring.

9. Which of these King of the Ring winners was granted a championship match at SummerSlam?

a. Owen Hart
b. Kurt Angle
c. Mabel
d. Brock Lesnar

10. The tournament took a four-year hiatus and returned in what year?

a. 2005
b. 2006
c. 2007
d. 2008

11. Which SmackDown general manager reintroduced the King of the Ring tournament?

a. Stephanie McMahon
b. Vickie Guerrero
c. Theodore Long
d. John Bradshaw Layfield

12. Which WWE superstar has been King of the Ring in two consecutive years?

a. Randy Savage
b. Bret "The Hitman" Hart
c. Mr. Ass
d. Kurt Angle

13. The first-ever tournament took place at which location?

a. Sullivan Stadium
b. Providence Civic Center
c. Nutter Center
d. The Spectrum

14. True or False: The King of the Ring is the fifth major pay-per-view for WWE.

15. Which of these superstars is the most successful African American King of the Ring?

    a. R-Truth
    b. Booker T
    c. Kofi Kingston
    d. Mark Henry

16. This superstar is generally regarded as the worst King of the Ring.

    a. Triple H
    b. Mr. Ass aka Billy Gunn
    c. Wade Barrett
    d. Tito Santana

17. True or False: Mable was the first person of color to win the King of the Ring tournament.

18. Only one of these superstars has been a King of the Ring?

    a. Eddie Guerrero
    b. John Cena
    c. Chris Benoit
    d. Ted Dibiase

19. True or False: Kurt Angle is one of two Olympic medalists also to be King of the Ring.

ANSWERS

1. B – 1985

2. C – 1993

3. C – Don Muraco

4. B – Harley Race

5. A – Owen Hart

6. C – The Awesome

7. B – Randy Savage

8. True

9. D – Brock Lesnar

10. B - 2006

11. C – Theodore Long

12. B – Bret "The Hitman" Hart

13. A - Sullivan Stadium

14. True

15. B – Booker T

16. B – Mr. Ass is also known as Billy Gunn

17. True

18. D – Ted Dibiase

19. False

CHAPTER 19:

HELL IN A CELL

TRIVIA TIME

1. When did the first pay-per-view edition of Hell in a Cell take place?

    a. 2007
    b. 2008
    c. 2009
    d. 2010

2. What WWE event did Hell in a Cell replace?

    a. Vengeance
    b. No Mercy
    c. No Death
    d. No Vengeance

3. About how many feet is the steel cage in which competitors compete in during Hell in a Cell?

    a. 15
    b. 16
    c. 19
    d. 20

4. The main event of the first Hell in a Cell took place between which superstars?

a. The Dudley Boys vs. The Hardy Boys
b. D Generation X vs. The Legacy
c. Evolution vs. The Hardy Boys
d. Kane vs. The Undertaker

5. Which WWE superstar has competed in the most Hell in a Cell matches?

a. Shawn Michaels
b. The Undertaker
c. Kane
d. The Big Show

6. Which Amerian city has hosted the most Hell in a Cell matches?

a. Chicago
b. New York
c. Dallas
d. Houston

7. Which WWE superstar has the most Hell in a Cell match wins?

a. The Undertaker
b. Kane
c. Mankind
d. Paul Bearer

8. How many different championships have been defended in Hell in a Cell?

a. 5
b. 6

c. 7

d. 8

9. Which of these superstars has served as a two-time special referee in a Hell in a Cell match?

    a. Triple H

    b. Shawn Michaels

    c. Kurt Angle

    d. Vince McMahon

10. Which superstar is known for taking the highest and riskiest leap from a steel cage?

    a. A. Shane McMahon

    b. B. Rey Mysterio

    c. C. Eddie Guerrero

    d. D. Chavo Guerrero

11. Which of these superstars has failed to win a single Hell in a Cell match?

    a. Randy Orton

    b. Mick Foley

    c. CM Punk

    d. Kane

12. When did the first-ever Hell in a Cell match take place?

    a. The 1980's

    b. The 1990's

    c. The 2000's

    d. The 2010's

13. Which two superstars competed in the first Hell in a

Cell match?

    a. Mick Foley and Kane
    b. Triple H and Kane
    c. Triple H and Shawn Michaels
    d. Shawn Michaels and The Undertaker

14. Which of these superstars was the first and only superstar to be pinned on top of the steel cage?

    a. Edge
    b. Christian
    c. Chris Jericho
    d. CM Punk

15. Which of these wrestlers interrupted the first-ever Hell in a Cell match?

    a. Mick Foley
    b. Kane
    c. The Big Show
    d. The Undertaker

16. The first time a title changed hands at Hell in a Cell resulted in which of these superstars becoming World Heavyweight Champion?

    a. Randy Orton
    b. The Undertaker
    c. John Cena
    d. Triple H

17. In what year did the first-ever title change hands at WWE?

    a. 2009

b. 2010

c. 2011

d. 2012

18. Which of these WWE superstars made use of a truck to rip out the door of a steel cage?

a. CM Punk

b. Shane McMahon

c. Vince McMahon

d. Triple H

ANSWERS

1. C – 2009

2. B – No Mercy

3. D – 20

4. B - D Generation X vs. The Legacy

5. B – The Undertaker

6. C – Dallas

7. A – The Undertaker

8. C – 7

9. B – Shawn Michaels

10. A – Shane McMahon

11. B – Mick Foley

12. B – The 1990's

13. D – Shawn Michaels and The Undertaker

14. C – Chris Jericho

15. B – Kane

16. B – The Undertaker

17. A – 2009

18. C – Vince McMahon

CHAPTER 20:

WWE TABLES, LADDERS, AND CHAIRS

TRIVIA TIME

1. Which year did the first T.L.C. event take place?

   a. 2007
   b. 2008
   c. 2009
   d. 2010

2. What month of the year does T.L.C. take place?

   a. September
   b. October
   c. November
   d. December

3. Which pay-per-view event did T.L.C. replace?

   a. Armageddon
   b. Vengeance
   c. Hell in a Cell
   d. Extreme Rules

4. True or False: Since its inception, all Tables, Ladders, and Chairs matches have been fought in indoor arenas.

5. Where was the first Tables, Ladders, and Chairs event hosted?

    a. Toyota Center
    b. Barclays Center
    c. Wells Fargo Center
    d. AT&T Center

6. True or False: WWE fans voted the concepts of the event.

7. There has only been one T.L.C. event not to take place in December. In what month was it held?

    a. September
    b. October
    c. November
    d. July

8. To win a table match, the opponent must?

    a. Submit
    b. Be pinned
    c. Be hit with a table
    d. Be put through a table

9. True or False: All weapons are legal during Tables, Ladders, and Chairs matches.

10. In a Chairs match, the traditional way to win is?

    a. By pinfall or submission
    b. By climbing a chair
    c. By hitting your opponent with a chair
    d. By using the most chairs

ANSWERS

1. C - 2009

2. D - December

3. A - Armageddon

4. True

5. D - AT&T center

6. True

7. B - October

8. D - Be put through a table

9. False

10. A - By pinfall or submission

DID YOU KNOW?

- In a Ladders match, the only way to win is by using the ladder to retrieve the item hanging above the ring.

CHAPTER 21:

WWE STUDIOS

TRIVIA TIME

1. WWE studios was founded in what year?

   a. 2001
   b. 2002
   c. 2003
   d. 2004

2. Who served as the first-ever president of WWE studios?

   a. Jed Blaugrund
   b. Vince McMahon
   c. Joel Simon
   d. Triple H

3. Which WWE superstar starred in the first theatrical film of the studio?

   a. John Cena
   b. The Rock
   c. Stone Cold Steve Austin
   d. Kane

4. Which popular WWE film has gotten up to five sequels?

a. *The Marine*
b. *12 Rounds*
c. *The Chaperone*
d. *The Condemned*

5. Which WWE superstar has a show named after themselves currently airing on Netflix?

   a. Triple H
   b. The Undertaker
   c. The Big Show
   d. Shawn Michaels

6. The WWE female TV show "Fight Like a Girl" is streaming on which platform?

   a. Prime Video
   b. Netflix
   c. Hulu
   d. Quibi

7. The WWE film titled *See No Evil* features which of these WWE superstars as the lead character?

   a. Kane
   b. The Undertaker
   c. Mankind
   d. The Big Show

8. Which of these films was the first-ever WWE film not to feature a WWE star as the lead?

   a. *The Chaperone*
   b. *That's What I Am*

c. *12 Rounds*

d. *No One Lives*

9. WWE films have collaborated with all but one of these popular cartoons to produce a feature.

   a. *Flinstones*

   b. *Scooby-Doo*

   c. *The Jetsons*

   d. *Samurai Jack*

10. True or False: WWE films have released a French feature film in the United States of America and Canada.

11. What is the highest-grossing WWE film?

    a. *The Rundown*

    b. *Walking Tall*

    c. *The Scorpion King*

    d. *See No Evil*

12. Which of these superstars played the lead role in the WWE comedy *Knucklehead*?

    a. Mark Henry

    b. The Big Show

    c. Goldberg

    d. Kane

13. Who is the highest-grossing WWE superstar of all time?

    a. Dave Batista

    b. Dwayne "The Rock" Johnson

    c. Hulk Hogan

    d. John Cena

14. Which WWE superstar has starred in the most films?

    a. John Cena

    b. Dave Batista

    c. Dwayne "The Rock" Johnson

    d. Hulk Hogan

15. Which of these WWE superstars is currently part of the Marvel Avengers franchise?

    a. Dave Batista

    b. John Cena

    c. Dwayne "The Rock" Johnson

    d. Triple H

16. Which of these WWE films was distributed by Netflix?

    a. *The Main Event*

    b. *The Marine*

    c. *12 Rounds*

    d. *Fighting with my Family*

17. A film about which of these WWE legends aired on HBO?

    a. Hulk Hogan

    b. Stone Cold Steve Austin

    c. Dwayne "The Rock" Johnson

    d. André the Giant

18. Which Late WWE superstar starred in the film *Mohawk*?

    a. Chris Benoit

    b. Eddie Guerrero

    c. Luke Harper

    d. Owen Hart

19. Which of these WWE superstars featured in the Christmas flick *Christmas Bounty*?

    a. The Miz
    b. Triple H
    c. John Cena
    d. Shawn Michaels

20. The 2018 film *Blood Brother* features which of these African American superstars in the lead role?

    a. Booker T
    b. R-Truth
    c. Kofi Kingston
    d. Mark Henry

21. Which of these superstars has not played the lead in *The Marine* series?

    a. John Cena
    b. The Miz
    c. Ted Dibiase Jr.
    d. David Otunga

22. Which of these superstars played the lead in the family-friendly film *The Chaperone*?

    a. Triple H
    b. Shawn Michaels
    c. Hulk Hogan
    d. The Big Show

23. WWE has had their films distributed more times by this company than any other company?

a. Universal Pictures
b. Lionsgate
c. Warner Bros
d. Metro Goldwyn Mayer

24. The film *The Interrogation* stars which of these two superstars as the lead?

   a. Miz and Maryse
   b. Booker T and Carnell
   c. Edge and Lana
   d. John Cena and Brie Bella

25. Where is the headquarters of WWE studios located?

   a. New York
   b. Chicago
   c. Washington
   d. Los Angeles

26. True or False: All films released by WWE star only WWE-signed superstars.

27. In 2014, WWE announced a six-film partnership with a company that has been dubbed the "Action Six-Pack Series." The deal was with which company?

   a. Warner Bros
   b. Sony pictures
   c. Disney
   d. Lionsgate

28. The A&E network will be producing documentaries for all but one of these superstars.

a. Vince McMahon
b. Bret Hart
c. Mick Foley
d. Ultimate Warrior

29. *12 Rounds* stars John Cena in the lead role. Which superstar played the lead in the sequel?

a. Daniel Bryan
b. Dean Ambrose
c. Roman Reigns
d. Randy Orton

30. The film *Pure Country: Pure Heart* stars which of these superstars in the lead role?

a. Kurt Angle
b. Mr. Kennedy
c. Shawn Michaels
d. Ted Dibiase

ANSWERS

1. B - 2002

2. C - Joel Simon

3. B - The Rock

4. A - *The Marine*

5. C - *The Big Show*

6. D - Quibi

7. A - Kane

8. B - *That's What I Am*

9. D - *Samurai Jack*

10. True

11. C - *The Scorpion King*

12. B - *The Big Show*

13. B - Dwayne "The Rock" Johnson

14. C - Dwayne "The Rock" Johnson

15. A - Dave Batista

16. A - *The Main Event*

17. D - André the Giant

18. C - Luke Harper

19. A - The Miz

20. B - R-Truth

21. D - David Otunga

22. A - Triple H

23. B - Lionsgate

24. C - Edge and Lana

25. D - Los Angeles

26. False

27. D - Lionsgate

28. A - Vince McMahon

29. D - Randy Orton

30. C - Shawn Michaels

DID YOU KNOW?

- WWE studios was formerly known as WWE Films. The name lasted from 2002 until 2008 when the name was changed.

- The first theatrical film released under the WWE films' name was *The Rundown* starring Dwayne "The Rock" Johnson, while the last theatrical release was called *The Condemned* and starred Stone Cold Steve Austin.

- The first-ever film starring a WWE (then WWF) superstar was *No Holds Barred* featuring Hulk Hogan in 1989. The film was released under the Shane distribution company and was released on DVD in 2012.

CHAPTER 22:

WWE VIDEO GAMES

TRIVIA TIME

1. In what year did WWE start releasing gaming apps?
   a. 2011
   b. 2012
   c. 2013
   d. 2014

2. The first-ever WWE game was published by which company in 1987?
   a. Take-Two Interactive
   b. Yukes
   c. MicroLeague
   d. Nintendo

3. What was the first WWE game released on PlayStation?
   a. WWE All-Stars
   b. W.W.F. Attitude
   c. WWE 2K13
   d. W.W.F. Rage in the Cage

4. In what year was W.W.F.'s No Mercy released for GameBoy color?

a. 2000
b. 2001
c. 2002
d. 2003

5. True or False: Since 2013, the *WWE 2k* series has become the official game for WWE and is published by Take-Two interactive.

6. What was the first-ever arcade-based WWE game released?

  a. *WWF Superstars*
  b. *WWE All-Stars*
  c. *WWE Battleground*
  d. *WWE Redemption*

7. In what year was the first-ever *WrestleMania* game released?

  a. 1987
  b. 1988
  c. 1989
  d. 1990

8. True or False: The first game based on Royal Rumble was released in 2010.

9. What was the first game to be released in the *SmackDown* series?

  a. *WWE SmackDown*
  b. *W.W.F. SmackDown*
  c. *W.W.F. SmackDown, Know your Role*

d. *WWE SmackDown, Know Your Role*

10. True or False: There is a game series known as *SmackDown vs. Raw*.

ANSWERS

1. C - MicroLeague

2. B - W.W.F. Attitude

3. A - 2000

4. True

5. A - W.W.F. Superstars

6. C - 1989

7. False

8. B - W.W.F. SmackDown

9. True

CONCLUSION

You made it! You have accompanied me on this nostalgic journey through so many iconic moments of WWE, and I hope it was a pleasing experience.

Without a shadow of a doubt, World Wrestling Entertainment (WWE) is one of the significant staples of entertainment, not only in the United States of America but globally.

The organization brought joy to its viewers and fans and popularized the sport of wrestling.

For decades, world stars have been made after coming through the WWE roster ranks into mega Hollywood stardom, leaving an impact in other fields.

WWE is here to stay, and for many more years, more memories will be created. I surely hope (and I believe you do, too) they will be positive ones.